THE THINGS WE SEE:

SHIPS

By David Pye

PENGUIN BOOKS · HARMONDSWORTH

NOTE TO THE READER

'Intended to be read, not skipped'

(Lecky : *The Danger Angle and Off-shore Distance Tables*)

The beauty of ships can be appreciated without technical knowledge of shipbuilding and the sea, just as the countryside can be enjoyed without an understanding of geology and agriculture. It would be a pity if we shut our eyes to everything we did not understand.

This book has been written for those who have little or no technical knowledge, and it is not meant to impart more than a few rudiments of it. The author is not a Naval Architect.

The illustrations include some brilliant photographs of splendid ships : but they are inevitably not a representative collection. They do not cover every type of ship or even the best ships of any one type. Not all the modern ships illustrated are still afloat.

The owners and builders of ships illustrated, and the owners of the copyright of photographs, are given in a list on pages 63 and 64.

ACKNOWLEDGEMENTS

I wish to thank the shipowners and shipbuilders who have kindly provided me with photographs ; and the Institute of Naval Architects, who, while in no way responsible for this book, allowed me access to their library. If I have claimed more or less for the Art of Naval Architecture than its exponents would have done themselves, I hope that the general sense of what follows will excuse any particular errors they may find.

THE COUNCIL OF INDUSTRIAL DESIGN

The Things We See : Ships is number 6 of a series of books undertaken as a result of suggestions made to the publishers by the Council, which has given a varying degree of assistance in preparing individual volumes. The opinions expressed in each case, however, are those of the author.

The Council was set up in December 1944 by the President of the Board of Trade to promote by all practicable means the improvement of design in the products of British industry. Inquiries from manufacturers, retailers and designers on any problem of design, and inquiries from all interested in promoting design-appreciation, are welcomed at Tilbury House, Petty France, London, S.W.1.

Made and printed in Great Britain for Penguin Books., Ltd., by Harrison & Sons, Ltd.

First Published 1950.

1 A modern Collier : The *Cormoat*

This book is about the appearance of ships ; and their appearance may seem a trivial matter compared with what they do. If they did not do their job we should go hungry, and if we were hungry we should be in no frame of mind to care what they looked like. The same argument can be applied to any number of things besides ships, and it is sound as far as it goes; so it would perhaps be reasonable before writing a book about the appearance of ships, to reply to this argument and explain why their appearance seems worth discussion.

Any adequate reply would fill a very much bigger book than this. A ship's appearance matters because, as the saying truly goes, 'It does you good to look at' a fine ship or anything else that is beautiful. Nearly all the things men design can be beautiful, and in spite of all that is said of modern ugliness, a great many of them still are. It is true that you can live a fairly satisfactory life without paying any attention to their beauty, just as you can without ever taking a holiday: but in either case you will have missed something that is wonderfully refreshing and would make life more satisfactory still. A handsome

3

ship and an ugly one may both be equally good at fetching us food, but the handsome one provides something else besides; which, if not a necessity, is much more than a luxury to anyone with an eye for it.

And any number of people would find they had an eye for it, if they would look, and put their mind to the shape of things as readily as they do to the tune of a song; instead of thinking about the purpose of the thing, or the value of it, or dismissing it from their mind because it is familiar, or letting it remind them of something else. Our trouble, surely, is not that 'we have no time to stand and stare,' but that we have forgotten how to do it.

A good designer, consciously or unconsciously, arranges the elements of a thing's shape—the edges, planes, hollows, curves, convexities, and the rest of them—to make something which appeals to us through the eye much as a tune appeals to us through the ear. He designs the thing, in fact, not only to do its job efficiently, but also to do it handsomely, and 'take the eye.' Thus according to the criterion applied throughout this book a thing must be beautiful as well as efficient if it is to be considered well designed: efficiency alone is not enough.

But what does the 'beauty' of a ship consist in ? and what 'good' does it do you to look at it ? There is no certain answer to either question; and since there is no short answer at all, none can be given here. The reader will have to satisfy himself by experience that ships are worth looking at: and it is at least unlikely that any answer yet given would directly enlarge his appreciation of their beauty. The best evidence we shall find that the appearance of ships is not a trivial matter, is this: that naval architects, shipbuilders, seamen and shipowners, who are not more inclined to trivialities than other people, have always thought a great deal of their ships' appearance.

It is a remarkable fact that in the last two hundred years few things of comparable importance have been as consistently well designed as ships; yet naval architecture has been held in little esteem as an art. We find, for example, wholesale condemnations of the Victorian age for the crudity and pretentiousness of its arts of design, and the fact that this age produced the *Ariel*, *Thermopylae*, *Cutty Sark*, *Taeping*, and hundreds of other ships less well known but no less beautiful, has seldom been put forward in its defence. It is true that the buildings of the Victorian age are still with us, whereas the ships are not, but I do not think that this alone accounts for the ships being disregarded. It is the fact that designers of ships have always been pre-occupied with what they must make their ships *do*, rather than with how they would like them to look, that accounts both for the high standard of ship design and also for the low esteem in which it has been held. If we examine this apparently paradoxical situation we shall find out a good deal not only about ships, but about contemporary architecture and industrial design of other kinds as well, where the same state of affairs very often obtains.

The process of designing a ship consists in producing a very carefully adjusted compromise which will both satisfy the needs of the ship's prospective owners and comply with the dictates of the sea. Any preconceived ideas or special preferences which the designer may have about the appearance of ships can be allowed to

2 The tea clippers *Taeping* and *Ariel*

affect the design only if they assist or at any rate do not prejudice the success of the compromise. It follows that the restrictions placed upon the designer by the owners and the sea at the outset, must weigh much more with him than any preferences of his own. We may take it, for example, that designers of ships have very seldom been able to square their shoulders at the start of a job and think to themselves —"Now we'll do something really original —like this" or "Now we'll sit down and produce a really fine imposing design" or any other of the famous first thoughts which have sometimes lured architects into committing a monumental disaster. The gist of their collective thoughts—for a team of men is needed to design even a small ship—might be rather more like this: "The requirements are that the ship shall carry so many tons of cargo; have so many cubic feet of cargo space; steam at so many knots; run so many miles without refuelling; and do several other things, all of which we shall have to provide for. It has yet to be decided whether the ship is to have steam or diesel engines, and the decision will depend on which is likely to be cheaper in the long run: that will have to be worked out. Very well, for a start we will make a guess, based on the experience we have gained from designing other ships which had similar requirements, and we will assume that a ship of this general shape and these dimensions will meet the requirements we are faced with now. A ship such as we are assuming will, by our calculations, displace so many tons of water; and if she is going to float at the draught we want, the ship with everything

5

in her will have to weigh the same number of tons, so now we will calculate the weight of the ship and her equipment, machinery and fuel, and add the weight of the cargo to be carried, and see if the total is the same. If not we shall have to adjust the dimensions we assumed at first and repeat the calculations until we find that our adjustments have made the dimensions meet the requirements."

There will follow calculations for stability, strength, cost and other things, all of which will have to be made before the design can be finally settled; and in determining the form of the hull and the power required to drive it, the designer may resort to tank tests with experimental models.

Furthermore, most of the requirements pull in opposite directions: for example, the fine-drawn hull, which is easily driven and gives speed with economy of fuel, because of its fineness also gives less cargo capacity than the broad hull with a bluff bow and heavy stern; but this more box-shaped hull, needing more power to drive it at the same speed, will have a larger proportion of its capacity taken up with machinery and fuel and will cost more to drive. The designer has to find the compromise between the two extremes that will pay the owner best, and it can hardly be a simple problem.

Again, any alteration in the requirements that is made while the design is developing will very probably affect the distribution of weight in the ship and hence her trim and stability—that is to say the attitude in which she floats and her power to regain her balance when rolling or pitching. A comparatively small alteration may have a considerable effect in

terms of weight: suppose that some alteration in the ship's equipment—or in wartime, her armament—required the addition of one or two men to the crew originally allowed for; then more accommodation would have to be provided, more food would have to be stored and cooked, more fresh water would be used, and so on. All this would take up space in the ship and involve extra structure to enclose the space, which in turn would add more weight, the total amounting perhaps to tons.

Some of the calculations on which the final design is based can be checked for certain only by comparison with known facts and figures derived from similar ships which have already been built and tried out at sea. If a radical innovation is made in the design there will be no similar ships in existence to provide a check, and the new ship's qualities may prove on trial to be worse or better than expected. Advances in ship design have on the whole been gradual rather than sudden and spectacular, not because naval architects have been excessively conservative, but because they have very rightly hesitated to risk seamen's lives, owners' money, and their own reputations in ships whose strength and performance they could not guarantee before they had been put to the test at sea. The evolution of each ship from her predecessors also explains the family likeness sometimes seen between ships designed by the same firm.

Considering how many other things have a prior claim on their attention and skill, we may well, as laymen, be surprised that naval architects do manage to give their ships' appearance the attention it deserves. The problem that confronts them

is very different from that confronting the designer of such things as furniture, pottery, or some kinds of buildings; where there may be fifty simple ways of satisfying the requirements, and where appearance is the designer's chief preoccupation. Thus, the requirements for a flower vase are, that it shall cost so much, hold the flowers and water, stand up, and be easy to clean. Any jam jar would meet the functional requirements; the problem is to make a vase which is as good to look at as the flowers in it.

There are, then, two widely different modes of design: one where the problem centres on requirements almost to the exclusion of appearance; one where appearance is the essence of the problem, and the designer can take the requirements in his stride. The first is typified by the modern ship or aircraft, the second by the medieval church or classical temple. Both modes—Design by Requirements and Design by Appearance—are equally capable of producing things that we call beautiful. There is no great gulf fixed between 'utilitarian' design by requirements and 'artistic' design by appearance, as though one were a lower order of activity than the other. The two are different in degree, not in kind; and the difference is simply that in one the designer has less freedom of choice than in the other.

It has sometimes been said that in the first the form of the object is determined by its function, while in the second it is determined by the designer's 'caprice,' and it has been even maintained that the first kind of design is 'right' and the second 'wrong.' But in practice the requirements that define the function of what is being designed merely enable the designer to determine the limits within which the shape of it may vary: within those limits the designer has no option, but chooses whatever shape his 'caprice' (or good sense) suggests. The function of an object may, it is true, be defined by requirements so exacting that, as for instance in the hull of a ship, only one form or a few comparatively slight variations of it can fulfil them in each case. But nearly always, as in planning a ship's accommodation, or a house, the designer can invent alternative arrangements each of which will fulfil the requirements; or perhaps no conceivable arrangement will perfectly fulfil them all, but several compromises are possible; and the designer, balancing their relative advantages and disadvantages, has to choose between them. In either case the designer has to make a choice; in the hull his freedom of choice is very limited, in the accommodation it is still limited, but less strictly.

If there is one certainty about the arts of design, it is that designers have always preferred to have limits set to their freedom of choice; and they find it intensely difficult to design shapes which satisfy the eye unless their freedom is limited. It is most interesting to speculate on the reasons for this; but whatever the reasons there is little doubt of the fact. When the requirements of function or the difficulty of manufacture have not set them close enough limits, then designers have adopted arbitrary limits instead, which had nothing to do with function: that is to say they have developed styles. Thus, in building, the ancient Greeks confined themselves to a construction of columns and beams of a few stereotyped forms—the 'Orders';

8

while Gothic builders favoured a system of pointed arches. Whatever the origin of such styles, they were in practice an effective convention for limiting the variety of shapes that the designer could use. The functional requirements for buildings in those days were comparatively easy to satisfy and did not provide their designers with the limits they needed.

In shipbuilding we do not find such clearly defined styles, for the requirements have always been difficult enough to satisfy without the designer denying himself any possible means of doing so; and if the form of ships has become stereotyped from time to time, this has usually been due to the pressure of requirements rather than style.

Very little external ornament has been applied to ships for many years past, because most of them have been built to earn money and their requirements have been framed to that end alone. If a ship is to compete profitably with her rivals her first cost must be low and the designer must dispense with ornament and most other things that do not directly contribute to satisfying the requirements: for it seems that handsome ornament no longer helps to attract a good crew, as it is said once to have done.

All that now remains of ornament is found in the design of the ship's scheme of paintwork: which involves little extra cost, since the ship has to be painted in any case, but which can add much to a ship's appearance by emphasising certain features of it. For example, in the *Normandie*, 84, the sheer was emphasised by the line where the white and black paint met along the side. Ships are usually painted with a few good strong colours and

5 The figurehead of the *Cutty Sark*

sharply contrasting tones, such as red, black and white, or black, buff and white. It is an excellent tradition.

In the old days solid ornament was obviously considered much more important and was used to evince the ship's prestige, 4, 5, 6, 44. Ship-owners found it necessary to set off the ship's personality with a neat figurehead and scroll work, just as their wives still find it necessary to be fashionably dressed. But the ornament was never more than adornment. Ornament could never make an ill-designed ship look handsome, though it might enhance the beauty of a fine one. Added ornament does not make, and may easily mar, good design. In his *Treatise on Naval Architecture* (1848) A. F. B. Creuze says that "the family of the Petts

6 The figurehead of the *Beatrice*

7 The *Scot*, 1891

were the great instrument in the improvement of the Navy . . . and it is probable that but for the taste for gorgeous decoration which prevailed during the seventeenth century, this ingenious family would have been able to effect much more": in other words, the prevailing style was too much for them and prevented them from meeting the requirements as well as they could have done without it. The ships 'took the eye' but did their job imperfectly.

Just as a style can become too much for the designer, so also can functional requirements. Indeed it is perfectly possible for requirements to be so intractable that a designer has the utmost difficulty in finding any satisfactory compromise which will meet them. Too little freedom of choice can be as fatal to good design as too much—more fatal in fact, because designers of outstanding ability can put up with

a great deal of freedom, but even they are helpless with none at all. It may be no fault of the designer's that a ship looks badly designed: it is his misfortune always to be judged by results: the public at large are not to know that he may have been asked to put a quart into a pint pot—nor that he may almost have succeeded!

There are probably some types of ship which are incapable of being made to take the eye, and anyone criticising a ship's design or her designer should remember this. Only an expert will be able to judge whether the designer's problem could be solved; and if so, whether he has solved it well.

To appreciate the beauty of good design, on the other hand, requires no expert knowledge; but it is one thing to appreciate it and quite another to explain what it is, how it is recognised and under-

8 The *Capetown Castle*, 1937

stood. The designer himself cannot explain the quality of his design. He arrives at a good design by choosing one set of shapes in preference to another, but he may be too much preoccupied with meeting requirements to be conscious that he is doing so; and even if he is conscious of choosing, he will not be able to give any real explanation of the mental process that decides his choice; for just as the mental process of logical reasoning can find expression in words but not in the notes of music, so can the mental process of designing find expression only in shapes but not in words. It is impossible to give a reasoned explanation of the beauty of design, simply because it is not the product of logical reasoning but of a different kind of thought. Looking at good design will help to understand it more than reasoning about it—or than reading about it. The

illustrations will speak for themselves better than I can speak for them.

There are qualities of good design which can be described; but it is not possible to point to a beautiful ship and a commonplace one and to say, "this one is beautiful *because* she has a pronounced sheer, which the other has not; or because she has a rounded front to the bridge, or a raking stem, or a flaring bow." A ship may have all these things and be ugly, or none of them and still be beautiful.

The ships built in the last seventy years for the Union-Castle Mail Steamship Company and its predecessors, The Union Steamship Company and Castle Mail Packets Company, 7–12, are an interesting demonstration of developments in the design of passenger liners during that time. Among them I suppose most people would agree that the *Capetown Castle*

9 The *Hawarden Castle*, 1883

10 The *Balmoral Castle*, 1910

11 The *Arundel Castle*, 1921

12 The *Arundel Castle* after alteration, 1937

and the *Scot* are both very beautiful, probably more so than the *Arundel Castle* as originally built. They are all three quite different from each other in appearance, yet the appearance of the *Capetown Castle* and the *Scot* has an effect upon us which that of the original *Arundel Castle* has not. But it would be vain to make a list of all the ways in which the two resemble each other more than they resemble the *Arundel Castle*, in the hope of isolating a common factor which accounts for their beauty. Such a factor may be there, but for lack of words to define it, it could not be put in the list.

Again, it will probably be agreed that the *Arundel Castle* after alteration, 12, is a finer looking ship than she was before. But no one could say precisely and certainly why two funnels and the new bow suit her better than four and the old one.

If anyone, hoping to discover what beauty there is in ships, reads this and finds it merely exasperating, then I repeat; let him look at the ships. In nearly every illustration in the book, something has struck me as beautiful. No one will agree with my taste in every case, but no one would maintain that none of these ships has beauty. If you find that any of them please you (or at least make you feel less exasperated) look at those, and never mind the rest. Really look at them, and afterwards keep looking for something else that pleases you in the same way. You will find it, in ships and other things; and soon you will find more things which please you than you did at first.

Good design is not the prerogative of any single type of ship or of ships of any one period. There are seamen still at sea who remember and lament the beauties of Sail, 13. There are likewise seamen now at sea who will probably live to remember and lament, in the days of their gas turbine driven or atomically-energised seniority, the beauties of Steam and Diesel, 14. They will do well to remember but they will doubtless be foolish to lament. There is no need to decry the modern ship because she has no sails—as though sails in themselves were a guarantee of beauty. Nor are Passenger Liners necessarily—or commonly—better looking than Cargo Liners, or Tramps, or Coasters, or any other kind of ship. (Perhaps it should be said that there is nothing derogatory about the term 'Tramp' as applied to ships. It means, in most cases, merely a ship that takes cargoes wherever obtainable and to any port, unlike a liner, that usually plies between the same ports.)

Most of the ships illustrated here were built fairly recently. Recent designs have been chosen because the last fifteen or twenty years seem to have produced more fine-looking ships than any period since the 1850s and 1860s when the famous clipper ships were built for the China trade. The naval architects of the present day seem to have mastered the problem of satisfying requirements to such a degree that they have about the right amount of freedom of choice when designing. If they had much more they would presumably have to develop a defined style. There would not necessarily be any harm in that, but there would be an added risk of things going wrong. Deliberately adopted styles can look attractive enough while they are still current but they have a way, once they go out of fashion, of becoming tiresome. It is interesting that the *Scot*, with her bow in the style of a sailing ship, has

13 . . . ' the beauties of sail '

14 . . . ' the beauties of steam '

15 Model of the passenger and cargo liner *St. Essylt*

not done this; perhaps because that kind of bow was still part of a living tradition of ship design when she was built.

In one of the latest and best looking ships in this book, 15, a distinct new style has begun to appear. The result is very striking; but fine though she is, I should like her as well with a funnel of the more usual form. The streamlined shape of *St. Essylt*'s funnel is pleasing in itself, and it is, no doubt, efficient; yet I feel that it has a character which, though right and necessary in aircraft which travel at two or three hundred miles an hour, is not perfectly in keeping with the character of the various interesting shapes in the upper works of ships which travel at fifteen or twenty knots.

In the present instance the designer, having adopted this style, has made a virtue of it. The *St. Essylt*'s streamlined funnel is a valuable element in the design because it successfully contrasts with other shapes in the ship, and its outline echoes the general silhouette of her midships superstructure. (These points are discussed further on page 19.) But it would be an evil day for naval architecture if designers who had less good taste took to "streamlining" the upperworks of ships wholesale, after the fashion which is so common in contemporary design.

Except for some warships and wartime cargo vessels, to which special considerations apply, ships have rarely been standardised as cars and aircraft are, for the sake of mass production. The demand for new ships, and the types of ship in demand, are not steady and predictable but fluctuate according to the state of world trade. Consequently mass production is rarely practicable and ships are still built to the individual owner's requirements. These may change by the time the company builds another ship, and one shipowner may not have just the same requirements as the next. But the requirements do not differ fundamentally in the same trade. Ships built for the same work are recognisably of the same type although each ship of the type will have been designed individually (unless she

16 The *Devis*, passenger and cargo liner

happens to have sister ships), and will differ from every other.

The first essential of good appearance in a ship is that she shall look a unified whole, not a collection of separate parts whose shapes are unrelated to each other. The ship must look 'all of a piece.' Nothing substantial can be removed from a good design without spoiling the look of what remains. The sister ships *Devis* and *Delane* will illustrate this point. Their designer obviously intended to make the several parts of the midships superstructure, together with the funnel, appear as one piece of architecture; and he has notably succeeded. The appearance of every part has been considered in relation to the appearance of the whole. It should be observed that in this photograph the *Devis* has a deck cargo of Diesel locomotives forward and aft, which being no part of the design could be removed without detriment to the ship's appearance.

This photograph also illustrates one inevitable exception to the rule that nothing can be removed from a good design without affecting it. The *Devis* as seen here is not fully loaded. If she were, her water line would be near the white line painted on her side. That is the trim in which she would most often go to sea and in which she would look her best. If a piece of paper is laid on the photograph with its edge along the load water line her appearance as a whole will gain by it. The same would be true of almost any other ship, and it is not surprising. It is doubtful whether a ship could be designed which looked equally good when light and load-

17 The *Delane*, passenger and cargo liner

17

18 The *Southern Wheeler*, whaler

19 The *Southella*, trawler

ed. But in compensation, the shape of a ship's hull can be seen to better advantage when she is light, even though her appearance as a whole is usually less satisfactory in that condition, at least when viewed from abeam. As a rule, a ship that looks good when light will look better still when down to her marks.

It will be apparent in any successfully unified design that several of the shapes in it have the same special character. In the whale-catcher *Southern Wheeler*, 18, for instance, the forward part of the vessel with its bold sheer and flaring bow would say, if any shape could speak, "I mean to lift over the waves: I shall not plunge down into them"; and the bridge, built like a tower, would say, "The sea may break over the deck but I shall stand fast and keep my head above it." Both express by their shape the same resolution to stand up to the sea.

But if all the shapes in a design were uniformly similar in character a certain monotony would result. When once we had seen it we should soon tire of it. Design needs an element of surprise to keep our interest in it alive: a little mustard or a grain or two of Cayenne pepper, however excellent the dish itself; something in fact to provide the spice of contrast, for lack of which the smooth and perfect shape of a fast aircraft or a projectile is liable to pall. In ships the element of contrast is seldom lacking. In the double-banked frigate, 20, for instance, the light, lofty spars and sails contrast with the low, heavy hull; and it is this contrast, as much as anything else, that makes her a delight to see. Her hull, in itself, looks uninteresting beside that of the trawler *Southella*, 19; a ship of comparable length, whose beauty

20 Frigate, from a contemporary drawing

also is enhanced by contrast—the contrast between the curving sweep of the hull and the square upright shape of the superstructure.

But one can have too much of contrast. Indeed in ships there can easily be too much; and if there is our attention will be drawn to the difference between shapes instead of to the relation between them, so that the unity of the design will be lost. In the *Southella* the curved front of the bridge softens the contrast between its squareness and the curves of the hull enough to prevent this loss of unity. The bridge as it were makes a concession to the hull by faintly echoing the shape of it; and by so doing draws attention to the relation between bridge and hull rather than to their difference from each other.

This echoing or repetition of one shape by another can be noticed in any successful design. Sailing vessels owe much of their beauty to it, where the curved surfaces of the sails echo the curves of the hull (and both contrast with the straight lines of the spars and rigging). The raking stem, which was often used in sailing vessels and is now again becoming common, satisfies the eye more than the straight (upright) stem which it is superseding, because it repeats the forward and upward trend of the sheer line—that steady upward sweep of the deck towards the bow which is a great part of the beauty of ships, and makes them look eager to go forward, reminding us how the bow lifts to take the ship over an advancing swell.

The several types of ship each have their characteristic beauty. The Liner's speed and multiplicity of accommodation give her a hull which is fine at the ends and high in the sides, with a flaring bow to give deck space on the forecastle and throw the sea clear as she cuts through it, 21. The concave section of the bow will contrast with the convex cruiser stern and the large expanse of unbroken side with the complexity of the long superstructure above it; whose many windows, stanchions, ventilators, and other relatively small units give the ship 'scale'; that is to say they make it evident how large the hull and funnel must really be if so many hundred man-sized objects can be ranged between them.

21 . . . . 'a passenger liner's characteristic beauty' : The *Athlone Castle*

22 . . . 'power and confidence' : the Dutch ocean-going tug *Thames*

The Tug, 22, expresses power and confidence in every line of its hull, like the prize-fighters in old engravings with broad heavy shoulders and deep chests, narrow in the hips and light on the feet.

Many cargo vessels of modern type show how a fine design may be made of the simplest elements—a short compact superstructure and upright funnel set on a long hull with the sheer line unbroken from stem to stern. There is no parade about them, yet they achieve great dignity, and the fact that so few and simple elements are involved draws attention to the intrinsic quality of each. The sheer may not be very steep, but its sweep is evident because it is unbroken. The spars may not be tall, but they look their full height because they stand in isolation and the eye is not distracted from them. The bow may look bluff and the stern full, but every curve of the hull is seen to its full advantage because the upperworks make a sufficient contrast without competing with it for our attention.

And so does every type have its characteristic failings where the design falls short of the best that can be done. The Liner may have a bow that looks too fine and quarters that look too heavy, with a

23 The *Saga* at sea. A Swedish North Sea passenger and mail liner   24 The *Saga* in harbour

bridge that towers up like a cliff, so that when the ship is seen from ahead, the bow, which should be proud, is made to look a meagre kind of snout; and when the ship is seen from abeam the super-structure will look so huge that it dwarfs the hull and will itself be dwarfed by monstrous funnels which destroy the 'scale' completely. Doubtless there has never been a ship so bad that this whole description could be fairly applied to her, but unsuccessfully designed ships of this type have usually exhibited a tendency to some such faults.

The faults of a badly-designed Tramp, on the other hand, will be so far negative that they escape definition. A bald, slab-sided hull that hangs in the water like a log instead of riding on it like a gull: a gaunt little bridge sitting on the middle of it: a funnel like a sawn-off length of pipe: and altogether a crude, clumsy look. But with all this, the ship will still have a sort of uncouth dignity, speaking of hard work in hard conditions and defying critical sneers.

No design can be seen in isolation. Whatever its merit, its effect will depend a great deal on the setting in which it is seen. A ship seen in a harbour, 24, and the same ship at sea, 23, strike the eye very differently. The open sea and sky in their infinite variety of light and colour provide a setting which from time to time will make a dull ship look splendid and a fine ship miraculously beautiful, 35. For a ship's design to be appreciated she ought to be viewed at sea, and moving, at such a distance that all of her can be seen at once, but not so far off that her shape becomes indistinct and her size insignificant—the disadvantage from which aircraft, in an equally magnificent setting, usually suffer when seen from the ground. But aircraft have this advantage in compensation, that the complete design can be seen at once: whereas the most beautifully curved part of a ship's hull is hidden under water, and can only be seen when the ship is building; or in dock; or in a model; or at moments when the motion of the sea lifts her forefoot or propellers clear of the water.

On the page opposite and the nine following it, there are photographs of some well-designed ships with comments on various aspects of their design.

25 Aerial view of the *Tyr*

The *Tyr*, 25, was a Norwegian tramp ship. In the photograph above she is seen with all her hatches open and appears to be discharging or loading her cargo, although there was evidently no work in progress at the moment when the photograph was taken. The work was apparently being done by the floating crane lying alongside her, and her own derricks are swung over to starboard out of its way.

The principal parts of the ship visible in the photograph are, starting from the bow: the forecastle head and the anchor windlass on it; then an open hatchway; and a mast with derricks rigged and winches at the foot of it for working them. Near them are some ventilators. Abaft this mast there is another hatch which cannot be seen because the bridge superstructure is between us and it. On top of this superstructure is the compass platform having a clear view all round the horizon for taking bearings, and round it is a framework for spreading an awning in a hot climate. Abaft the bridge is another hatch with twin derrick posts like short masts standing close to it and abaft them again is another superstructure with an awning spread and the small funnel coming through the awning—a small funnel because this is a motor ship. The lifeboats can be seen below the edge of the awning.

Next comes the after well deck, in all respects like that between the forecastle and bridge, and over the stern is the poop on which can be seen a deckhouse with more awning framework round it and a small docking bridge on top of it from which the after part of the ship's side can be watched as she comes alongside. Abaft this is the hand emergency steering gear and the ensign staff over the ship's name.

26 The Admiralty rescue and salvage tug *Hesperia*

The *Hesperia*, above, is a salvage tug built for the Admiralty during the late war, in which she and other tugs of the same type formed part of the escort of convoys and helped to save damaged ships.

There are three main kinds of tugs: those which like the *Hesperia* are designed for ocean towage and salvage work; those which tow ships in and out of harbours or narrow channels and help them to berth; and the smaller tugs which tow lighters in harbours and partly sheltered waters, as in the illustration opposite.

All tugs however large (and the *Hesperia* is very large, as the man on the forecastle shows in this picture), have the same kind of silhouette, high forward and low aft. All the after part of the ship has to be kept low so that the tow rope can pass from side to side across it when the tug and the ship towed change their relative positions. The tow must be made fast near the middle of the tug, for a ship towing from her stern finds it as difficult to manœuvre as a dog does if held by his tail.

It can also be seen in the photograph that there is nothing that the tow rope could foul or catch on, and nothing that it could chafe against. If it did either it would be weakened; and no rope, whether made of wire or manilla hemp, is too strong for a powerful tug with a heavy tow.

24

27 Tug and lighters in the Thames

Tugs when berthing a ship sometimes work by pushing with their bow against the ship's side, and carry a large rope fender or cushion round their stem to protect themselves and the ship. Similarly, the *Hesperia* has a large belting round her side to protect it when alongside a damaged ship or a wreck. She is provided with everything that could be of use at such a time including fire fighting equipment with a foam-making plant, salvage pumps, and a hospital.

The photograph on this page shows one of Messrs. Everard's tugs towing a pair of lighters, craft which depend either on tugs or the tide to move them. Lighters are used chiefly for shifting cargo from place to place in ports—the Port of London has a good forty miles of wharf in it—and ships often discharge their cargo into lighters direct.

There is perhaps nothing very striking about lighters in the Thames or anywhere else, unless we except those in Norway which have retained the same identical model as Noah's Ark, roof and all. But there is a considerable fascination about the approaches to any large port, where such craft and their tugs are often to be seen. They provide incident in a kind of seascape to which nearly every painter of the sea has been attracted.

28 The Collier *Wallsend* at sea

The *Wallsend*, 28, is a collier and the *Crane*, 29, a " short sea trader"; types of ships which, like coasters, spend much of their time in home waters.

There is a line about a "dirty British Coaster" which has been often quoted. Coasters and colliers have more frequent opportunities of getting dirty than most ships, it is true; but this only goes to show that they often take more trouble about keeping clean, for some of them are smart enough. It is fair to add that in this, if nothing else, the British weather helps them. The sea washes them down quite as assiduously as the crew. Ships with two low well decks doubtless came to be known as "three island ships" for that very reason. In small vessels of the type, the superstructures can become islands indeed, when the sea washes across the well decks between them in heavy weather.

The three island type of silhouette is a very usual one, and innumerable different versions of it are to be seen, the *Wallsend's* being as neat an example as any. The *Crane's* profile on the other hand is of a rather unusual type. She has two hatches before the main superstructure and only

29 The *Crane*, a cargo ship in the short sea trade

one abaft it, with the result that the funnel is about one third of her length from the stern instead of being nearly amidships, or, as in the majority of coasters, quite close to the stern. Having no forecastle the fore deck looks still longer than it otherwise would, but the bold sheer gives her enough freeboard at the bow to satisfy the demands of appearance and also of efficiency. If she had no sheer she would be liable to take a great deal of water over the bow in bad weather.

The *Crane's* one concession to ornament —the white streak along her side—is painted so as to draw attention to this sheer, and shows how much can be done with such an apparently simple device if it is used in the right way. It is interesting to speculate how something of the same kind could have been done in the *Wallsend*, and what the effect would have been. A modern ship, after all, is invisible. Only the coat of paint that hides her can be seen. So there are occasions when the design of the paintwork counts for nearly as much as the shape of the ship inside it; the *Wallsend's* fine shape is perhaps emphasized by her sober coat of black.

30 The *Kronprins Frederik*

The ships above and opposite are the *Kronprins Frederik*, a ship carrying mail and passengers across the North Sea, and the *Cubahama*, a fast ship which was built for fruit carrying. They are both remarkably smart to look at and they are interesting to compare because the effect is achieved in a different way in each case.

It is evident at a glance that the design of the *Kronprins Frederik* has been influenced by a definite style; a thing which, as has already been said, is in itself neither good nor bad. Whether or not we prefer the less stylised *Cubahama*, we shall, I think, agree that the *Kronprins Frederik's* design succeeds. Like all skilful work it looks easy: as though

there were no other possible way of treating such a ship. Her superstructure has a family likeness to some of the better modern cars and aircraft and shares with them a style whose influence is increasing in many fields of design. It has been suggested that future developments on these lines may result in ships whose whole intricate superstructure will be enclosed in a "fairing" much as some machinery is enclosed and hidden in a smooth cover.

If this idea does come to be applied generally to ships, their character may undergo as great a change as it did when sail gave way to steam. Developments in the design of motor car bodies suggest that a new departure of this kind would give as many opportunities for bad design as for good. In the hands of a good designer the "fairing" might be as clean and lively as the hull itself, but handled by an insensitive man it could look flashy and obese.

In the *Cubahama* there is nothing reminiscent of the style which emerges in the *Kronprins Frederik*. The *Cubahama's* design also is conspicuously successful, but here no attempt has been made to smooth the complexity of the upperworks. They rather serve as a foil to the smoothness of the hull. The curve of the bridge front and the sweep of the bulwarks up to it and the forecastle and poop, unify the design by preventing the contrast between the hull and upperworks from telling too harshly.

If the bows of the two are compared it will be seen that while their profiles are alike, the shape is not the same in both. The *Cubahama's* stem is relatively sharp and consists of a steel bar along which the plates of the two sides are brought together in a wedge form. The *Kronprins Frederik* has instead of the bar, a curved plate separating the plates of the two sides. If the latter had been prolonged till they met in the same fashion as the *Cubahama's*, they would have given a long overhanging profile not unlike the *Scot's*, 7, a "Clipper's bow" of the kind which we associate with figureheads. It is interesting to see that the broad curve of the plate which forms the *Kronprins Frederik's* stem also provides a site for a figure-head, none the less.

31 The *Cubahama*

32 The *Mauretania*

The measurements of the *Mauretania*, 32, and *Nieuw Amsterdam*, 33, are about 772 feet long and 35,700 tons gross for the first, and about 758 feet long and 36,287 tons gross for the second. That is to say they are much smaller than the *Queen Elizabeth* and *Queen Mary*, but still of the very largest size; and their appearance at close quarters is majestic enough.

They each have a very clean silhouette, and the photograph of the *Mauretania* shows how compact and regular in outline her superstructure has been made. In the appearance of both, an important part is played by the sheer line, and it is emphasised to the greatest possible degree by the meeting of the dark and light paint. The strong contrast between the tones attracts the eye to this line and it at once suggests speed and easy movement.

The raking masts and funnels also contribute to the same impression. It is not easy to understand why they do so unless it be from the idea of their having been swept back by the wind of the ship's passage. The device of raking spars to give an impression of speed, smartness and fierceness is a very old one, and in some ships, notably the early American Baltimore Schooners, it was taken to extraordinary lengths, being considered to improve their sailing qualities.

33 The *Nieuw Amsterdam*

The rake gives a sense of direction as well as of movement. The eye is drawn towards the bow rather than the stern as by an arrow pointing to it. If there were no rake the silhouette of both these ships would be nearly symmetrical, and each half would comprise one funnel and one mast: each half would be about equally interesting and there would be nothing to draw the eye decisively towards one end of the ship rather than the other, nor would there be anything at the middle of the ships' length, between the two equal halves, for the eye to rest on (a third funnel for example). In such a case a certain indecision in the design would be felt because of the duality of interest. It is the rake on the funnels and masts which prevents this from happening in these two ships.

In both ships the overall effect of the design is achieved by the same few lines, the sheer, the raking masts and funnels, and the overhanging profile of the bow and stern. But in each of the two a perfectly distinct character is apparent. Their appearance differs in this respect in much the same indefinable way that the face of a Dutchman might differ from that of an Englishman.

34 A motor tanker, the *Regent Panther*

The *Regent Panther*, above, is a tanker; and has the type of silhouette characteristic of nearly all such ships: a long hull having a raised forecastle, bridge, and poop, and with the engines and funnel right aft.

A tanker's hull is simply a gigantic tank, subdivided and stiffened internally, and formed in the shape of a ship. The ship *is* the tank. Sea water touches the outside of her plates; and oil, or whatever liquid she may carry, touches the inside of them. The same hull has to contain the engines (and the boiler furnaces as well, if the ship is propelled by steam.) Being placed in the stern they can be isolated from the oil by a coffer-dam or watertight compartment; and this, together with the fact that hot gasses as they rise from the funnel will usually blow clear astern without having to pass over any part of the tanks, reduces the risk of fire and explosion to a minimum.

The accommodation for officers and crew is contained in the superstructures, and when the ship is at sea access from one to another is made easier by a fore and aft bridge, such as can be seen in the *Regent Panther*, running the length of the ship.

35. Training ship *Deutschland*

THE HULL

The shape of the hull and other component parts of a ship are well worth examination separately. As to the hull: in slow cargo vessels the bulk of it is comprised in a parallel middle body shaped like a long box, flat at the bottom and having nearly flat vertical sides, with the corners between bottom and sides rounded off. There is nothing of particular interest about the appearance of the middle body itself. It is at the ends of the ship and at the transition between the parallel body and the ends that the shape becomes interesting. As they run towards the ends the flat planes of the middle body first gradually and then distinctly become curved, and unite to form the characteristic shapes of a ship's bow and stern, 40. The resulting double curvature is perfectly smooth but not geometrically regular: it looks more like a naturally formed than a man-made shape: it has the kind of continually changing curve we see in a flame, a snow-drift, a sea shell, or the body of a fish: it looks alive.

In fast ships the parallel body becomes quite short in proportion to the whole length, while in small vessels and some warships it disappears and the curvature runs continuously from bow to stern so that the hulls of these vessels often have the most lively and pleasing shapes of any, underwater. In olden days the idea that a ship's underwater body ought to resemble a fish was evidently favoured, 36,

and there are models of vessels of the seventeenth, eighteenth and early nineteenth centuries, which have a shape very like the belly of a fish with a keel growing out of it, 37. 'Cod's head and mackerel tail' (or 'gurnard's head' in Cornwall) was the term for them. A vessel with pleasing easy lines is still occasionally called 'as clean as a smelt.'

The hull has varied in shape at different periods, but the live character of its curves has always been apparent, sometimes approximating to the true streamlined shape of a fish, sometimes to the modern form with a less bluff bow; since a ship's body, moving half in air and half in water, takes a different shape from the body of a fish swimming all under water, or of a bird or aircraft in the air. The longer and finer the hull of a ship the faster can she be driven through the water, and ultimately the speed of the vessel will be limited by its length, unless it is made to rise and plane over the water as a flat-bottomed vessel will do if it can be driven hard enough: such as a sailing dinghy running before a fresh breeze, or a motor torpedo boat, 58.

Considering that ships are measured by the thousand tons and are hove about and battered by the sea in a way that no building could possibly withstand in an earthquake, the structure of their hulls is astonishingly light. They must be built with strength enough, but they must not

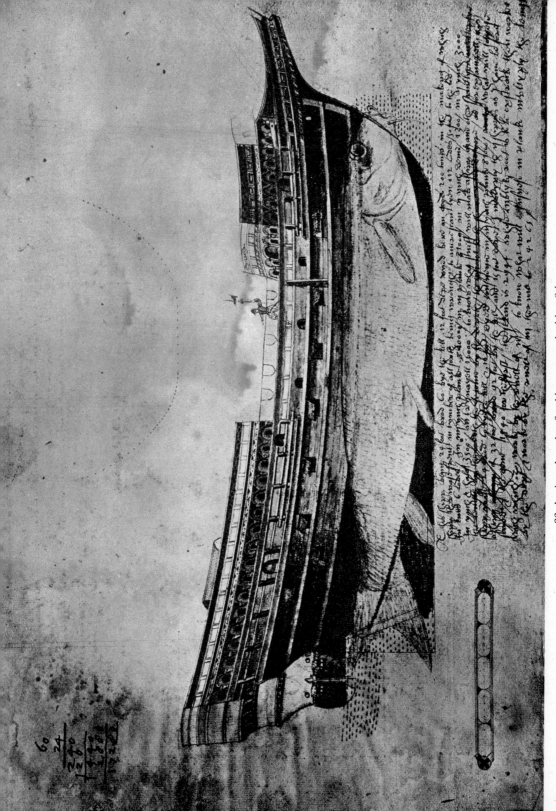

36 Ancient draught of a ship compared with a fish

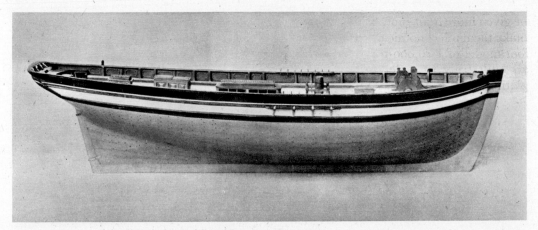

37 Buoy yacht of 1820–30

38 Motor launch building

be given more than enough, for that would make them uneconomically heavy. A four-foot model of a 10,000-ton ship, if it were all built truly to scale, would have side plating no thicker than stiff paper.

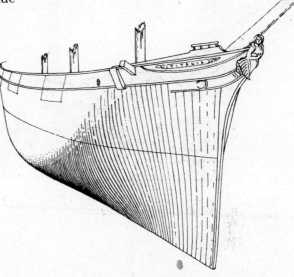

40 Sketch after a contemporary photograph of the *Titania*, clipper ship, in dry dock

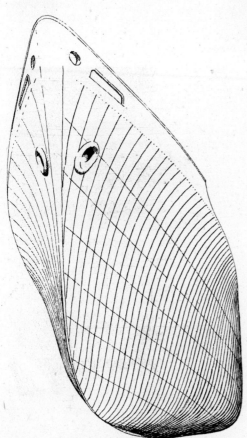

39 Sketch after a photograph of *Pozarica*, fruit carrier

(*overleaf*)
41 Bow of the *Aquitania*, built 1914
42 Bow of the *Stirling Castle*, built 1936

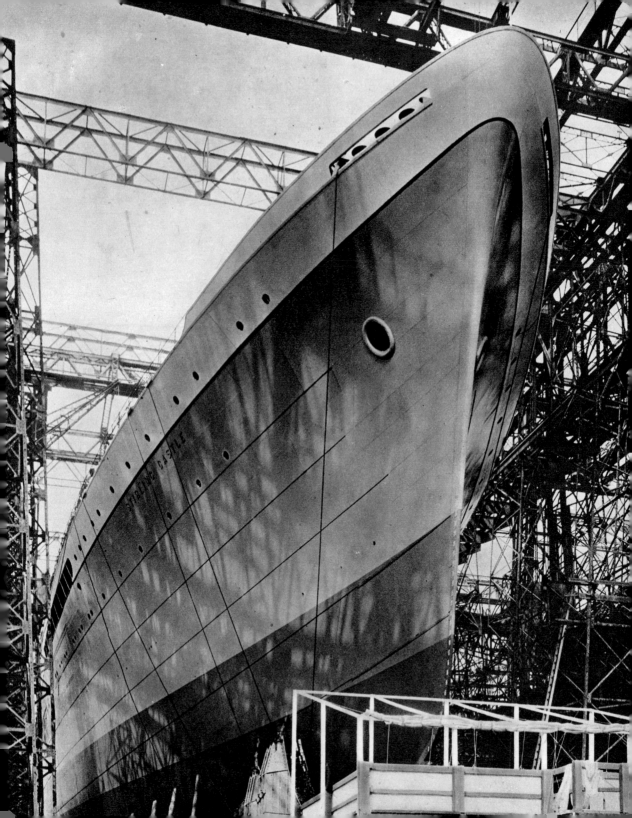

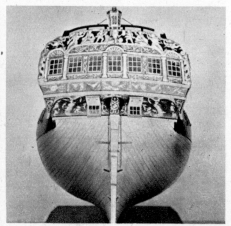

43 Stern of the *Queen Elizabeth*, 1940

44 Stern of a 44-gun ship of 1774–86

45 Model of 38-gun frigate, 1780–82

46 The *Windsorwood*, tramp ship, and

47 The *Patricia*, pilot cutter

UPPERWORKS

The upperworks of different ships show a far greater variety of forms than their hulls. There is a family likeness between the hulls of the wooden ships of a hundred years ago and the steel-built ships of today, but little or none between the upperworks of the two periods, 43–47. The special character of the architecture in the superstructure of a modern ship is something which has grown up in about the last seventy years, and nothing else is quite like it. The bridge, deckhouses, alleyways, bulwarks, rails, ladders, derricks, winches, bollards, ventilators, and the rest of what meets the eye on the decks of a modern ship, 51, have made a new vocabulary of shapes which speak of the sea quite as surely as the masts, yards, sails and gear of sailing ships used to do, 52. The words are different but the tone of voice is the same.

48 Deck view of the *Orion*, passenger and mail liner

49 The *Queen Elizabeth* in wartim

50 Painting a drifter's funnel

51 . . . 'the decks of a modern ship'

52 The four masted barque L'Ave

INTERIORS

No reference has yet been made to the interior of a ship. The interior decoration of ships is a subject about which much could be written, but I think it is one that should be considered separately from their general design. There is no essential difference between the problem of designing a room in a ship and a room anywhere else; and I shall go no further into the subject than to suggest that a style of decoration which has something of the directness found in the architecture on deck might be more appropriate to the public rooms of a passenger liner than the elaborate styles that are sometimes used.

53 Wheelhouse of the *Orion*

54 The *Conte di Savoia*

55 Bridge of the *Or*

WARSHIPS

There are two more branches of ship design that must find a place in however small a book on the subject. These are, the design of Warships and the design of small craft.

Some of the most important advances in the theory of naval architecture have been made by designers of warships, and peaceful trade must owe them a considerable debt. Their problems are more formidable than those which confront the designers of merchant ships, since the fundamental requirements for warships are particularly difficult to reconcile amongst themselves, and new requirements constantly arise as new weapons and methods of fighting develop.

There are some fundamental requirements, however, which have always been peculiar to warships; such as those Sir Walter Raleigh mentions: "that she be swift: that she be stout sided: that she carry out her guns all weather." And there are some defects to which apparently they have always been prone: for he says again: "The high charging of ships it is that brings them all ill qualities." The expression 'top-heavy' doubtless originated at sea, and top weight is anathema to Naval Constructors: in warships it tends constantly to increase because of alterations and additions to the armament and the gear which belongs to it, most of which has necessarily to be placed high in the ship; and if it increases too far the ship will "sinck deep into the water, labour and overset."

In spite of the overwhelming pressure of requirements on their designers, which might lead us to expect an opposite result, many modern warships are extremely handsome, 56–59, though it must be admitted that the appearance of many others suffers badly from the tendency of the upperworks to become crowded with the profusion of intricate gear that modern war requires. The chief beauty of most of them is, as might be expected, in the shape of the hull, which in outward appearance at least has not recently been subject to radical alterations, and so has a comparatively steady tradition of development behind it.

Aircraft carriers, 56, may be only the first of many new and strange types of vessel evolved to meet the hideous requirements of war; and H.M. Ships *Hood*, 57, and *Cossack*, 59, may represent the best of a tradition of design which began with the first ironclads and may even now be ending. The Motor Torpedo Boat, 58, no less good looking, will serve as a reminder that whatever war may wish to make of ships, the sea will have the last word in their design. The smallest ship may be the fastest and may carry weapons enough to sink the largest; but she must cross the sea to use them. In heavy weather she will break herself to pieces if she attempts to steam at the same high speed as the big ship.

57 H.M.S. *Hood*

58 One of H.M. Motor Torpedo Boats

59 H.M.S. *Cossack*

SMALL CRAFT

Nearly all that can be said of good design in ships applies equally to small craft, and there is of course no line of demarcation between the two. "One hundred foot long and five and thirty broad," says Sir Walter Raleigh, "is a good proportion for a great ship." Nowadays a hundred feet makes a very small ship indeed: the Naval M.L.s of the late war were longer and so are many of the tugs that look so small beside a passenger Liner; yet we say 'as big as a house': not many houses are more than 'one hundred foot long and five and thirty broad.' Ships in fact—even the smallest—are a great deal bigger than they seem.

Small craft are particularly interesting because there is still a great diversity of local types among them, whereas ocean-going ships long ago developed an inter-

60 International 14 foot dinghies

61 Model of Yorkshire Coble

62 Fishing vessel *Girl Pat*

national character. This could hardly have been otherwise, for as soon as an advance in naval architecture was made in one country, it was advertised abroad by every foreign-going ship in which it was embodied. But a great many small craft work in coastal waters and seldom enter ports outside the locality where they were built, so that their local characteristics do not get anything like the same advertisement. These local characteristics are partly determined by local requirements; the deep draughted fishing boats which work out of small harbours in South Cornwall, would not do on the North-East coast where the boats may have to be launched from a beach before they can put to sea, 61; but there is very little doubt that local prejudice formerly helped to preserve differences between the boats of places where working conditions were alike. If this had not been the case local types would hardly be dying out as rapidly as many of them are: the use of motors instead of sails, and the introduction of new methods of fishing would not alone explain their disappearance. Some of the modern vessels that are replacing them are very fine; but who would not wish to have seen the days when there were

63 Drifters putting to sea

64 American fishing schooner *Gertrude L. Thebaud*

65 Yachts on a beach

66 Brixham trawlers racing

67 40-foot motor yacht

68 Gondolas

55

boats working from every coast which had as much individuality as the harbours they sailed from and the men who sailed them?

Many British local types of the last hundred years have disappeared entirely, and many more are nearly gone, yet several still remain in service, some with sails replaced by motors, but some unchanged. Among the finest of them all are the Thames Spritsail Barges, 69. It was said ten years ago that these would also soon have disappeared, but they did great service in the War, and it may be hoped that they will be with us some time yet. Abroad there are many local types still to be seen, of which the smallest are often the most interesting—and efficient. Gondolas, 68, for example, are perfectly suited to plying in the smooth waters of narrow or congested canals, although their beauty is more often remarked on than their efficiency.

There are some types of small vessel which vary comparatively little from port to port, such as small tugs, launches, and particularly yachts, 70–72, the design of which is now almost as much internationalised as that of ships; though there are still fine yachts which have been converted from sailing fishing boats or from such vessels as the Bristol Channel Pilot Cutters.

Many yachts are designed simply for racing and are not intended to stay at sea for days together, and the smallest of these, sailing dinghies, are as beautiful as any, 60. One could almost believe that 14-foot dinghies might one day be collected like old violins, for the beauty of their shape and colour and surface. The best of them are built with almost as much exactness as violins. Their skin is not much thicker than a violin's belly, and like violins they

57

69 The *Veronica* and other Thames spritsail barges racing

71 The *Erivale*, ocean racing yacht

72 *Dragon* class racing yachts in a calm

combine the greatest strength with lightness.

Perhaps the most interesting development of modern Yacht design is found in the boats intended for off-shore or ocean racing, 71. They represent a very skilful compromise between the qualities in a boat that make for greater speed and those that make for greater ability to keep the sea and keep going in bad weather; with which they must be able to contend, because the races they sail often keep them at sea for several days. They are small and look frail and delicately rigged, but this is an illusion; and it is not surprising that they can be sailed about the open ocean, for no wooden vessels have ever been built more perfectly than the yachts of the last fifty years, and small size is no hindrance to seaworthiness; as witness the Royal

70 The *Britannia* as a 23-metre racing yacht (Beken & Son, Cowes)

73 The R.N.L.I. Lifeboat *Caroline Oates Aver and William Maine*. (Station : Ferryside, S. Wales)

National Lifeboat Institution's lifeboats, 73, which being as perfectly built as any yacht, and still more strongly, are able to withstand the utmost fury of the sea.

It is not altogether inappropriate that such a book as this should end with the mention of lifeboats. Ships can be works of art; but works of art are made for men, to enlarge the possibilities of human experience, not to provide a pleasant way of escape from life. It is a good thing to realise that ships are beautiful, but it ought also to be remembered that without the persistent courage of generations of seamen their beauty would never have been. The sea is pitiless. To design a ship is to challenge it, and to take a ship to sea is to offer battle. It is hardly possible to look at a lifeboat without remembering this. In years of war, ships' lifeboats must have contained every extreme of fortitude, endurance, agony, bitter despair, and hope and joy, that is possible to man.

SOME COMPARISONS

74 The *Pathfinder*, pilot cutter 1906   75 The *Columba*, paddle Mail Steamer, 1878

Old fashioned and distinguished

76 The *João Alvarez Fagundes*, trawler   77 The *Raunala*, tanker and ore carrier

Dissimilar size and work, similar character of appearance

78 The *Edea*, fruit carrier   79 The *Eros*, fruit carrier

Fruit carriers as a type are particularly graceful

80 The *Clan Cumming*, cargo liner   81 The *Nonsuco*, general cargo and vegetable oil

Good designs with a fairly simple silhouette

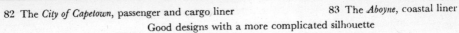

82 The *City of Capetown*, passenger and cargo liner   83 The *Aboyne*, coastal liner

Good designs with a more complicated silhouette

84 The *Normandie*   85 The *Unden*, general cargo

LIST OF ILLUSTRATIONS

(O) Owners and/or managers. (B) Builders. (C) Owners of copyright of photographs.

Where ownership has changed, the owners named are, in most cases, those who had the ship at the time when the photograph was taken.

42 (O) Union Castle Mail S.S. Co. Ltd. (B, C) Harland & Wolff Ltd.

43 (O) Cunard White Star Ltd. (B) John Brown & Co. Ltd. (C) Keystone Press Agency.

44 (C) By courtesy of the Director, Science Museum, S.W.7.

45 (C) By courtesy of the Director, Science Museum, S.W.7.

46 (O) Joseph Constantine S.S. Line Ltd. (B, C) R. & W. Hawthorn Leslie & Co. Ltd.

47 (O) Hon. Corporation of the Trinity House. (B, C) Smith's Dock Co. Ltd. Photo : W. Haig Parry, Middlesbrough.

48 (O) Orient S.N. Co. Ltd. (B) Vickers Armstrongs Ltd. (C) Stewart Bale Ltd., Liverpool.

49 (O) Cunard White Star Ltd. (B) John Brown & Co. Ltd. (C) Black Star.

50 (C) Fox Photos.

51 (C) Keystone Press Agency.

52 (O) Gustaf Erikson. (B) Rickmers A.G. (C) Fox Photos.

53 (O, C) Orient S.N. Co. Ltd. (B) Vickers Armstrongs Ltd.

54 (O) Societa Di Nav. Italia. (B) Cant. Nav. del Adriatico. (C) Associated Press Ltd.

55 (O, C) Orient S.N. Co. Ltd. (B) Vickers Armstrongs Ltd.

56 (O) H.M. The King. (C) Imperial War Museum, Lambeth Road, S.E.1.

57 (O) H.M. The King. (B) John Brown & Co. Ltd. (C) John Abrahams, Portsmouth.

58 (O) H.M. The King. (B) Camper & Nicholson Ltd. (C) Beken & Son, Cowes.

59 (O) H.M. The King. (B, C) Vickers Armstrongs Ltd.

60 (B) Uffa Fox and Others. (C) Bryan Westwood, Weybridge.

61 (C) Crown copyright.   Exhibit in Science Museum, S.W.7.

62 (O) Girl Pat Ltd., Grimsby. (B) George Ellery, Lowestoft. (C) Topical Press Agency.

63 (C) Associated Press Ltd.

64 (C) Associated Press Ltd.

66 (C) Fox Photos.

67 (B, C) Vosper Ltd., Portsmouth.

68 (C) David Soutar, West Ferry, Dundee.

69 (O) F. T. Everard & Sons Ltd., and others. (C) Associated Press Ltd.

70 (O) H.M. King Edward VII (when Prince of Wales) (Designer) G. L. Watson. (B) D. & W. Henderson, Glasgow. (C) Beken & Son, Cowes.

71 (O) Dr. Gordon Greville, M.C. (Designer) Robert Clark. (B) Sussex Yacht Works.

72 (Designer) Johan Anker. (C) John A. Stewart Clynder, Helensburgh.

73 (O) The R.N.L.I. (Designer) G. L. Watson. (B) Groves & Gutteridge Ltd. (C) Fox Photos.

74 (O) Hon. Corporation of the Trinity House. (B, C) Smith's Dock Co. Ltd. Photo : W. Haig Parry, Middlesbrough.

75 (O) David MacBrayne Ltd. (B) J. & G. Thomson, Clydebank. (C) Donald B. MacCulloch, Glasgow.

76 (O) Soc. Nacional dos Armadores de Bacalhau. (B, C) Cia União Fabril Lisboa. Photo : Seccão Fotografica de C.U.F.

77 (O) Grangesberg-Oxelösund Trafik A/B. (B, C) Aktiebolaget Götaverken.

78 (O, C) Cie Cyprien Fabre. (B) Ch. et Ateliers de Provence. Photo : Marcel Audry, Marseille.

79 (O) Erin S.S. Co. Ltd. (Bk C) Harland & Wolff Ltd.

80 (O) The Clan Line Steamers Ltd. (B) Greenock Dockyard Co. Ltd. (C), Nautical Photo Agency.

81 (O) North Negros Sugar Co., Manila. (B, C) William Doxford & Sons Ltd. Photo : Frank & Sons, South Shields.

82 (O) Ellerman Lines Ltd. (B, C) Cammell Laird & Co. Ltd. Photo : W. Ralston, Glasgow.

83 (O) Aberdeen Newcastle & Hull Steam Co. Ltd. (B, C) Caledon Shipbuilding and Eng. Co. Ltd. Photo : Norman G. Brown, Dundee.

84 (O) Cie. Gle. Transatlantique. (B) Ch. et Atel. de St. Nazaire. (C) Associated Press Ltd.

85 (O) O. F. Ahlmark & Co., Karlstad. (B, C) A. G. Lindholmens Varv.